Minibeasts In the Home

Sarah Ridley

A+

Smart Apple Media

Smart Apple Media
P.O. Box 3263, Mankato, Minnesota 56002

U.S. publication copyright © 2010 Smart Apple
Media. International copyright reserved in all
countries. No part of this book may be reproduced
in any form without written permission from the
publisher.

Printed in the United States

Published by arrangement with the
Watts Publishing Group Ltd, London.

Library of Congress Cataloging-in-Publication Data

Ridley, Sarah.
    In the home / Sarah Ridley.
        p. cm. -- (Where to find minibeasts)
    Includes index.
    Summary: "Profiles many insects and
invertebrates found in the home, discussing their
eating habits, habitats, and survival skills"--Provided
by publisher.
    ISBN 978-1-59920-328-7 (hardcover)
    1. Household animals--Juvenile literature. 2.
Arthropod pests--Juvenile literature. I. Title.
    QL49.R525 2010
    592'.1754--dc22
                                        2008045873

Series editor: Sarah Peutrill
Art director: Jonathan Hair
Design: Jane Hawkins
Illustrations: John Alston

Picture credits and species guide:
front cover t: Girls with Common house spider (*Tegenaria gigantea*), Tony Walters/PD. **b:** Palmetto cockroach (*Periplaneta americana*), Marcus M Jones/Shutterstock. **2:** Common House spider (*Tegenaria gigantea*), Warwick Sloss/Nature PL. **3:** Carpet beetle (*Anthrenus verbasci*) larva, John Downer/OSF. **6t:** Common House spider (*Tegenaria gigantea*), Sunset/FLPA Images. **6b:** Common Furniture beetle (*Anobium punctatum*), Richard Becker/FLPA Images. **7:** Common house fly (*musca domestica*), James H Robinson/OSF. **8t:** Silverfish (*Lepisma saccharina*), Michael Pettigrew/Shutterstock. **8b:** Pill woodlouse (*Armadillidium vulgare*), Richard Ford/Digital Wildlife. **9:** Palmetto cockroach (*Periplaneta americana*), Marcus M Jones/Shutterstock. **10t:** Common housefly. (*Musca domestica*), Stephen Dalton/NHPA. **10b:** Common housefly (*Musca domestica*) larvae and pupae, Anthony Bannister/NHPA. **11:** Common housefly (*Musca domestica*), Nigel Cattlin/FLPA Images. **12t:** Common House spider (*Tegenaria gigantea*), Warwick Sloss/Nature PL. **12b:** Common House spider (*Tegenaria gigantea*) and prey, Stephen Dalton/NHPA. **13:** Common House spider (*Tegenaria gigantea*) and spiderlings, Jean-Claude Teyssier. **14t:** Adult bed bug (*Cimex lectularius*), Nigel Cattlin/FLPA Images. **14b:** Clothes moth (*Tineola biselliella*) larva, Nigel Cattlin/FLPA Images. **15:** European dust mite (*Dermatophagoides pteronyssinus*), Sebastian Kaulitzki/Shutterstock. **16t:** Common wasp (*Vespula vulgaris*), Marty Kropp/Shutterstock. **16b:** Common wasp (*Vespula vulgaris*) nest, Nigel Cattlin/FLPA Images. **17t:** Common wasp (*Vespula vulgaris*) grubs, David Hosking/FLPA Images. **17b:** Death-watch beetle (*Xestobium rufovillosum*), David Hosking/FLPA Images. **18t:** Woodworm beetle (*Anobium punctatum*) larva, Nigel Cattlin/FLPA Images. **18b:** Furniture beetle (*Anobium punctatum*), B Borrell Casals/FLPA Images. **19t:** Photomicrograph of the common flea (*Ctenocephalides*), Carolina K Smith/Shutterstock. **19b:** Carpet beetle (*Anthrenus verbasci*) larva, John Downer/OSF. **20:** Girls with Common house spider (*Tegenaria gigantea*), Tony Walters/PD. **21:** Shoe box, Colin & Linda McKie/Shutterstock. **21c:** Kitchen paper roll, pixelman/Shutterstock. **21b:** Common woodlice (*Oniscus asellus*), Martin B Withers/FLPA Images. **22t:** Moth, Neil Bromfield/istockphoto. **22b:** Crane fly (*Nephrotoma quadrifaria*), Emily May Walden/istockphoto. **23t:** Green lacewing (*Chrysoperla carnea*), Stephen Dalton/NHPA. **23b:** Mosquito (*Culicidae sp*), yxowert/Shutterstock. **24:** Multicoloured Asian ladybirds (*Harmonia axridis*), Phototake Inc/OSF. **25b:** Millipede (*Diplopoda class*), Milos Luzanin/Shutterstock. **31:** Moth, Neil Bromfield/istockphoto.

The measurements for the minibeasts in this book are typical sizes for the type of species shown in the photographs. Different species within groups vary in size.

9 8 7 6 5 4 3 2 1

Contents

Minibeasts at Home   6

Under the Sink   8

Through the Kitchen Window   10

Hanging From the Ceiling   12

And Now to Bed   14

Up in the Roof   16

Under your Feet   18

Looking at Minibeasts   20

Summer Visitors   22

Winter Visitors   24

Identification Guide   26

Glossary   28

Web Sites to Visit   29

Index   30

Words in **bold** are in the glossary on pages 28–29.

Minibeasts at Home

Some minibeasts make their homes in our homes. Others visit in search of food or shelter, or come in by accident.

House Habitats

This spider's body can grow up to ¼ inch (1 cm) long.

▲ A house spider rests on a computer keyboard.

There can be several different types of **habitats** in a home. Under a sink it can be dark and damp. In the corner of a room it can be dry and warm. These habitats attract different minibeasts. Crumbs of food, carpets, and our belongings can become their food.

▶ Sometimes furniture beetle **larvae** become "bookworms," eating holes through the pages.

What is a Minibeast?

Minibeast is the name given to thousands of small **animals**. Although many are **insects**, others are not. Minibeasts do not have **backbones**, so scientists call them **invertebrates**. The ones that you are most likely to find in houses include spiders, wasps, flies, moths, ladybugs, woodlice, cockroaches, and silverfish.

TOP TIP!

Look out for boxes like these because they will help you become a good minibeast spotter.

Friends or Enemies?

Some minibeasts in our homes are **pests**, but many are harmless. A few are useful. House spiders catch small flying insects, such as flies and mosquitoes, which we don't want inside. Hungry wasps and flies land on our food and may spread diseases. Other pests include beetles that eat the wood in our homes.

This housefly can grow up to ⁵⁄₁₆ inch (0.8 cm) long.

◀ A housefly enjoys a plum. Flies like to eat our food.

Under the Sink

Sometimes it is damp under the sink in the kitchen or bathroom. It is also dark and this kind of habitat attracts certain minibeasts.

Speedy Silverfish

If you turn on the kitchen light in the evening, you might spot silverfish running for cover. These slim, silver insects have existed for 400 million years. In our homes, they eat spilled flour, photos, and even the glue that sticks wallpaper to the walls.

This silverfish can grow up to ¾ inch (1.8 cm) long.

▲ Silverfish are wingless insects, with three long "tails" at the end of the body.

▼ The hard shell of the woodlouse protects the soft body inside.

Harmless Woodlice

Woodlice are harmless, **nocturnal** animals. They eat crumbs of food, flakes of dead skin, and even their own droppings. Unlike the silverfish, they are **crustaceans** instead of insects, and have 14 legs.

The pill woodlouse can grow up to ⅝ inch (1.5 cm) long.

This American cockroach can grow up to 1.8 inches (4.5 cm) long.

Cockroach Pests

During the day, cockroaches rest around pipes, under floorboards, or under the sink. Then at night, they come out in search of food. They eat anything—meat, cheese, flour, pasta, and bread. Cockroaches will even eat each other if there is nothing else around.

▲ Cockroaches carry dirt and disease on their feet and then spread it onto our food.

There are more than 4,000 types of cockroaches worldwide and only 30 of them are pests. Cockroaches were around before the dinosaurs and were tough enough to survive the events that killed the dinosaurs.

9

Through the Kitchen Window

Leave the kitchen window open in the summer and flies are sure to buzz in. They can smell food and are looking for a good meal.

◀ A housefly flies towards a slice of bread.

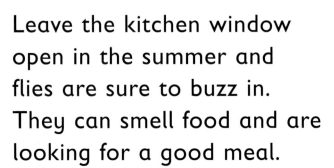

A housefly can develop from egg to adult in seven to ten days. The female lays eggs in trash, uncovered food, or a compost heap. The larvae hatch and feed on whatever is close by. After a few days they turn into **pupae**, and then into adult flies.

▲ The fly larvae are white; the pupae are red-brown.

Food of All Sorts

Houseflies have mouths that are like sponges, soaking up liquid food. The problem for us is that they are not fussy and they eat rotting food or even animal droppings. When they move on to our food, their feet leave small bits of dirt and **bacteria** on what we are about to eat.

▶ These houseflies are feeding on uncovered ham. It is important to keep food covered to stop this from happening.

TOP TIP!

If you see flies buzzing around a compost heap or a trash can, there may be fly larvae inside. Don't touch— just look at them.

Hanging From the Ceiling

Spiders are **arachnids**. They can surprise us by dropping down from the ceiling or running across the floor. Spiders eat flies, mosquitoes, and other insects that we do not want in our homes.

This spider's body can grow up to ¾ inch (1.8 cm) long.

▶ House spiders often fall into the tub by accident and then cannot escape.

Spinning a Web

A house spider has special body parts that make silk. The spider uses them to weave a web. Here it waits for an insect to walk or fly into the web. The insect sticks to the web and the spider injects it with poison.

◀ The spider feeds by sucking all the blood and juices out of its victim.

TOP TIP!

House spiders like to be left alone. Search for them in garden sheds, attics, or basements, as well as the corners of rooms.

Spiderlings

When a female spider has met a male to mate with, the female lays eggs in a sac and attaches it to her web. When the eggs hatch, tiny spiderlings come out. After a few days, they spin fine silk lines that carry them away to new homes. The male stays with the female for a few more weeks and then dies. The female sometimes eats him!

▲ A house spider protects its sac of spiderlings.

The harvestman is also an arachnid. It rests under windows or on walls during the day and then goes off hunting at night. It eats insect larvae and other small insects, dead or alive.

13

And Now to Bed

Some minibeasts are very unwelcome in our homes, especially the ones that like to live in our beds.

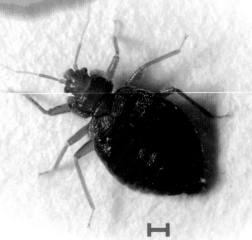

This bed bug can grow up to ³⁄₁₆ inch (0.5 cm) long.

Biting Bugs

Like all **bugs**, bed bugs are insects with special mouths for sucking. During the day, bed bugs hide away in bedding or behind the walls. At night, they crawl onto the sleeping person, bite through his or her skin, and suck up some blood. The bites are irritating, but not dangerous.

▲ These oval brown insects move into bedrooms by traveling inside suitcases, clothing, or bedding.

Another unwelcome minibeast in our bedrooms is the clothes moth. You are likely to see this small, brown moth in the summer months. The adult is harmless, but it lays eggs on carpets, clothes, or curtains. When the eggs hatch, the larvae (caterpillars) eat the fabric they are on, making holes.

This clothes moth larva can grow up to ³⁄₁₆ inch (0.5 cm) long.

14

Dust Mites

Most dust mites are too tiny to see without using a magnifying glass or **microscope**. These arachnids feed on flakes of dead skin that drop off our bodies all the time. Dust mites leave droppings behind them, and it is the droppings that make some people itch or wheeze.

▼ This photograph of a dust mite has been magnified—made much bigger than real life.

This dust mite can grow up to 1/125 inch (0.2 mm) long.

Up in the Roof

Up in the roof of a house, you may find an amazing wasps' nest or signs of boring beetles.

The Nest Begins

Many types of wasps live alone, but others live in huge colonies, or nests. The **queen** starts the nest by choosing a good site, such as a roof space. She builds a small nest, lays some eggs and feeds the larvae when they hatch. The larvae turn into worker wasps which build the nest bigger and bigger. They also fetch food for the larvae that hatch from the queen's eggs.

This wasp can grow up to ¾ inch (1.8 cm) long.

▼ Left undisturbed, wasps may build a huge nest in a roof space.

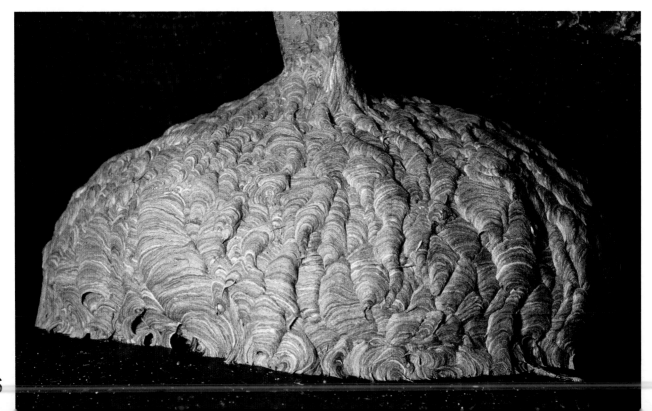

The Nest

The wasps build their nest from paper. They scrape off bits of wood from fences, outdoor furniture, or trees. They chew the wood and mix it with spit to make a paper **pulp**. The workers use the pulp to build hexagonal (six-sided) cells. Layers of paper pulp protect the cells on the outside.

▲ Each hexagonal cell contains one hungry larva that will turn into an adult wasp.

TOP TIP!

Many beetles and their **grubs** live in dead or dying trees. Look under the bark of fallen trees to see if you can see them, or the holes they have left behind.

This death-watch beetle can grow up to ⅜ inch (1 cm) long.

Wood Eaters

The death-watch beetle lays its eggs in the wood beams that hold up our homes. When the larvae hatch, they tunnel through the wood, eating it as they go. They can cause a lot of damage and can even make the building unsafe.

◄ An adult death-watch beetle comes out of a hole it has made in some wood.

Under Your Feet

You will rarely see the tiny minibeasts that live in carpets and floorboards, but you may feel them sometimes.

Woodworm

Woodworms are not worms at all, but the larvae, or grubs, of the furniture beetle. These small, brown beetles lay their eggs in wood. When they hatch, the larvae start eating out tiny tunnels through the wood—often our floorboards or furniture.

▲ A woodworm tunnels through a floorboard.

This woodworm can grow up to ¼ inch (0.6 cm) long.

This furniture beetle can grow up to ⅛ inch (0.3 cm) long.

▶ People rarely see the adult furniture beetle.

Hopping Fleas

The carpet on top of floorboards can get unwelcome visitors. These include insects called fleas. Fleas live on or close to pet dogs and cats. Sometimes they live in the carpet and hop onto whichever animal passes by— the cat, the dog, or even you! They bite into the skin and suck out blood. As fast as they arrive, they hop off again.

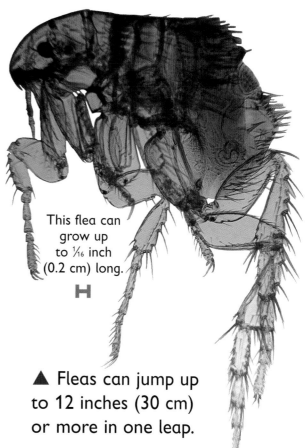

This flea can grow up to 1/16 inch (0.2 cm) long.

▲ Fleas can jump up to 12 inches (30 cm) or more in one leap.

Woolly Bears

The larvae of the carpet beetle are also called woolly bears. While the adult beetle feeds on plant **pollen**, the larvae like to eat wool carpets and other fabrics.

This carpet beetle larva can grow up to 1/8 inch (0.4 cm) long.

▲ A woolly bear eating a rug.

In the summer, look out for ants running around the floor. They are usually just visiting in search of fallen crumbs of food. They carry the food back to their nest to feed hungry ant larvae.

19

Looking at Minibeasts

Take a closer look at some of the minibeasts in your home or school by following these instructions.

You will need:
- Small plastic containers • A small paintbrush
- A magnifying glass • Paper and a pencil

What to do:
- Gently sweep any minibeasts in your home into plastic containers, using your paintbrush.

- Take a good look at each minibeast. How many legs does it have? Does it have wings? What color is it? Use the magnifying glass to take a closer look. The identification guide on pages 26–27 may help you to name the minibeast.

- You could draw the minibeast or write down its size, number of legs, wings, or **antennae.**

- Remember to return the minibeast to its home.

▼ Watch how a minibeast moves. Spiders can move very quickly on their long legs.

Wandering Woodlice

Woodlice prefer to live in damp places. Try out this activity to test this fact.

You will need:
- A shoebox with a lid, or similar container • Paper towels
- Water • A pencil • Woodlice

What to do:
- Take the shoebox and place a layer of damp paper towels in one corner of the box.

- Make small holes in the lid with the pencil.

- Find some woodlice. Good places to search for them are under stones or logs, in compost heaps, under garden pots, or in your house, if they live there.

- Gently place the woodlice in the shoebox, replace the lid and leave them for a few hours.

- Lift up the lid and see where the woodlice are resting.

Summer Visitors

There are far more minibeasts around in the summer than the winter (see page 24–25). Some of them find their way into our homes by accident.

Moths and Light

Moths fly through open doors and windows by accident on summer evenings. Confused, they often fly around as they try to find their way out again. If you open the window and turn off the light, they may fly outside again.

▲ A moth flutters around a light bulb.

This crane fly's wingspan can grow up to 1 inch (2.5 cm) wide.

Daddy Long Legs

Daddy long legs are really called crane flies. They are harmless flies that find their way into our homes by accident. Crane flies live for only a week or two. They mate, lay eggs in the ground, and then die.

◀ Crane flies have long, thin legs that can fall off if touched.

Delicate Lacewings

The pale-green lacewing is an insect with long antennae. Attracted by the light, it comes into homes. It is completely harmless and is useful in the garden because it eats up plant-wrecking **aphids**.

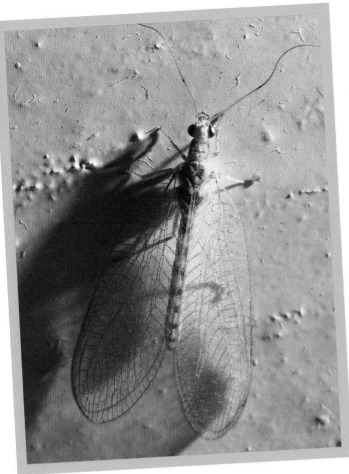

 This lacewing can grow up to ¾ inch (2 cm) long.

◀ You can see the veins in the lacewing's wings.

Munching Mosquitoes

Mosquitoes are unwelcome visitors to our homes. They fly into our bedrooms in search of a meal of human blood. Their sharp mouthparts pierce the skin so they can suck up blood.

▼ Only the female mosquito feeds on blood.

This mosquito can grow up to ¼ inch (0.6 cm) long.

Winter Visitors

Many minibeasts lay eggs and then die at the end of the summer. Others **hibernate** underground, inside plant stems, or find their way into our homes.

These ladybugs can grow up to ³⁄₁₆ inch (0.5 cm) long.

Lines of Ladybugs

Ladybugs can live for a year or two. They hibernate over the winter to survive. As the weather grows cooler, ladybugs search for a dry, warm place to rest. This can be along windowsills or inside cracks in our homes.

▲ If you find hibernating ladybugs, it is best to move them to a garden shed. In our warm homes, they are likely to wake up before spring and then die of hunger.

TOP TIP!

In winter you may see lacewings and some types of butterflies also looking for somewhere dry and warm to spend the winter.

1. Egg

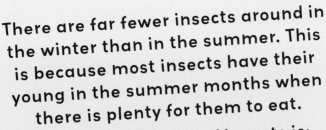

2. Larva

There are far fewer insects around in the winter than in the summer. This is because most insects have their young in the summer months when there is plenty for them to eat.

The usual **life cycle** of insects is: egg, larva, pupa, and adult. Look at page 10 for information about the life cycle of a housefly.

As the weather cools in the autumn, some types of insects hibernate while most die off, leaving eggs or larvae to survive them through the winter.

4. Adult

3. Pupa

Millipedes

Millipedes sometimes wander into our homes in search of shelter. They are completely harmless and do a good job outside by eating dead plant material and helping it to rot down. Although their name means "a thousand legs," millipedes usually have several hundred.

▼ There are several different types of millipedes but this snake millipede is the type that you are most likely to see inside homes.

The snake millipede can grow up to 1 inch (2.5 cm) long.

Identification Guide

The minibeasts in this identification guide are organized in the order in which they are featured in the book. Other common minibeasts are listed at the end. There are thousands of different minibeasts, so you may need to use a field guide, too.

Silverfish: This insect has a slim, silvery body covered in scales, and three long "tails" at the end of its body. It is nocturnal.

Harvestman: A harvestman is an arachnid. It is not an insect and it is not a spider. A spider has two body parts, while a harvestman has one.

Woodlouse: The woodlouse is a crustacean and has 14 legs and a hard, shiny body.

Bed bug: This insect sucks human blood, while other types of bugs suck **sap** out of plants or blood out of other insects.

Cockroach: The cockroach has a shiny red or brown body with long antennae. There are thousands of different types of cockroaches.

Dust mite: A dust mite is a tiny arachnid. It has eight legs and eats dead skin.

Fly: There are thousands of different types of flies. They are all flying insects with one pair of wings. Use a field guide to identify the type.

Wasp: A wasp is a flying insect with two pairs of wings. If wasps feel in danger they will sting, so don't touch!

Spider: Spiders come in all shapes and sizes but they all have eight legs and a body in two parts. They are arachnids.

Beetle: There are thousands of different beetles. They are all insects and many can fly. Some eat flower **nectar**, others eat other minibeasts, and some eat dead wood.

Beetle grub: A grub is the young of a beetle. The woodworm is the name of the grub of the furniture beetle.

Mosquito: The mosquito is a type of fly. The female feeds on animal blood and lays its eggs in water.

Flea: This tiny, wingless insect lives by sucking blood from animals. It usually lives in animal fur.

Ladybug: The ladybug is a flying insect with two pairs of wings. It is a small beetle that eats aphids.

Ant: An ant is a small insect with long antennas. It is related to the wasp and the bee and spends most of its time collecting food to take back to its nest.

Butterfly: The butterfly is a flying insect. It lays eggs that hatch into caterpillars. In time, the caterpillars turn into adult butterflies.

Moth: A moth is a flying insect and is similar to the butterfly. It lays eggs that hatch into larvae, also called caterpillars.

Millipede: The millipede is not an insect but belongs to the same group of animals as the centipede. It eats dead plant material and moves fairly slowly on its many legs.

Daddy long legs: This type of fly is also called a crane fly. It has very long legs, hence its name!

Earwig: The earwig is a small, shiny insect that lives usually in dark, damp places such as cracks in wood or walls, or under a stone.

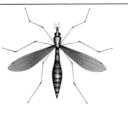

Lacewing: This pale-green insect has long antennas and almost see-through wings. It eats aphids and other small insects.

Headlice: The headlice is a tiny insect that lives in human hair. It feeds on human blood and lays eggs in hair.

Glossary

Animals A huge group of living things including birds, insects, mammals, crustaceans, reptiles, and amphibians.

Antennae Feelers on an insect's head and used for smell, taste, and touch.

Aphid An insect that sucks sap out of plants.

Arachnid An animal with eight legs, like a spider, harvestman, or mite.

Backbone The line of bones down the middle of the skeleton.

Bacteria The smallest forms of plant life that live everywhere—in soil, water, air, and inside our bodies. Some bacteria cause diseases.

Bug The name for an insect with piercing mouthparts, which it uses to suck sap from a plant or blood from an animal.

Crustacean A member of a large group of animals including woodlice. Most other crustaceans live in the sea—crabs, lobsters, and shrimp, for example.

Grub The larva of the beetle.

Habitat A place where plants and animals live.

Hibernate To spend the winter in a state of deep sleep.

Insects A huge group of animals. All insects have a body in three parts: the head, thorax in the middle, and abdomen at the other end. Six legs are attached to the thorax and many insects also have wings.

Invertebrates A huge group of animals without a backbone including insects, worms, and spiders.

Larva (plural larvae) The stage in the life cycle of many insects after they hatch from eggs.

Life Cycle The lifetime of a living thing, from birth until death. An insect life cycle often goes through these stages: egg, larva, pupa and adult.

Microscope An instrument that makes very small things appear bigger.

Nectar The sweet liquid made by flowers and eaten by many insects.

Nocturnal Animals that rest during the day and are active at night.

Pest An unwanted insect or other animal.

Pollen A fine powder made by the flower of a plant. It fertilizes other flowers.

Pulp A soft, soggy mixture, used to make paper.

Pupa (plural pupae) Part of the life cycle of many insects before they turn into adults.

Queen In wasps and colonies, the most important insect that lays all the eggs.

Sap The liquid inside a plant.

Web Sites to Visit

http://www.coolbugstuff.com/
Visit this site and learn more about the world of bugs through cool bug facts. Send a bug ecard and even look at a new way to find bugs in the home: through bug recipes.

http://www.pbs.org/wnet/nature/alienempire /metropolis.html
Find out more on termites and how they infect homes.

http://www.ars.usda.gov/is/kids/insects/ insectintro.htm
Click on different links to read about bug stories and news articles.

Note to Parents and Teachers:
Every effort has been made by the publishers to ensure that these web sites are suitable for children, that they are of the highest educational value, and that they contain no inappropriate or offensive material. However, because of the nature of the Internet, it is impossible to guarantee that the contents of these sites will not be altered. We strongly advise that Internet access is supervised by a responsible adult.

Index

animals 7, 8, 10, 11, 19, 27, 28, 29
antennae 20, 23, 26, 27, 28
ants 19, 27
aphids 23, 27, 28
arachnids 12, 13, 15, 26, 28

bacteria 11, 28
bed bugs 14, 15, 26
beetles 6, 7, 16, 17, 18, 19, 26, 27, 28
butterflies 24, 27

carpets 6, 14, 18, 19
caterpillars 14, 27
cockroaches 7, 9, 26
crustaceans 8, 26, 28

daddy long legs (crane fly) 22, 27
dust mites 15, 26

earwigs 27
eggs 10, 13, 14, 16, 17, 18, 22, 24, 25, 27, 28, 29

fleas 19, 27
flies 7, 10–11, 12, 22, 25, 26, 27

floorboards 9, 18, 19
food 6, 7, 8, 9, 10, 11, 16, 19, 27

grubs 17, 18, 27, 28

habitat 6, 8, 28
harvestman 13, 26, 28
headlice 27
hibernation 24, 25, 28

insects 7, 8, 12, 13, 14, 19, 23, 25, 26, 27, 28, 29
invertebrates 7, 28

lacewings 23, 24, 27
ladybugs 7, 24, 27, 29
larvae 10, 11, 13, 14, 16, 17, 18, 19, 25, 27, 28, 29
legs 8, 20, 22, 25, 26, 27, 28
life cycle 10, 25, 28, 29

millipedes 25, 27
mosquitoes 7, 12, 23, 27

moths 7, 14, 22, 27
mouthparts 11, 14, 23, 28

nocturnal minibeasts 8, 26, 29

pollen 19, 29
pupae 10, 25, 29

roofs 16–17

silverfish 7, 8, 26
sinks 6, 8–9
skin 8, 14, 15, 19, 23, 26
spiders 6, 7, 12–13, 20, 26, 28
summer 10, 14, 19, 22–23, 24, 25

walls 8, 13, 14, 27
wasps 7, 16–17, 26, 27, 29
windowsills 13, 24
wings 20, 22, 23, 26, 27, 28
winter 22, 24–25, 28
woodlice 7, 8, 21, 26, 28
woodworm 6, 18, 27
woolly bears 19